How Advertising Works

The Amazing Adv[...] of the GOB Mob and [...] From Oww[...]

D1249866

by David Fowler
Illustrated by John Nez

MONDO

To Mom and Dad
—D.F.

To ideas that always seem crazy at first
—J.N.

Text copyright ©2007 by David Fowler
Illustrations ©2007 by John Nez
under exclusive license to Mondo Publishing

All rights reserved.

No part of this publication may be reproduced, except in the case of quotation for articles or reviews, or stored in any retrieval system, or transmitted in any form or by any means, electronic, mechanical, photocopying, recording, or otherwise, without written permission from the publisher.

For information contact:
Mondo Publishing
980 Avenue of the Americas
New York, NY 10018

Visit our website at www.mondopub.com

Photo Credits: Cover © Douglas Peebles/CORBIS; 5: © Franco Vogt/CORBIS; 8: l. © CORBIS; r. © Swim Ink 2, LLC/CORBIS; 9: © Henry Diltz/CORBIS; 10, 15: © Ogilvy & Mather; 11: © Bob Rowan; Progressive Image/CORBIS; 12: © Kellogg Company; 16: © John Henley/CORBIS; 19: © Randy Faris/CORBIS; 21: b. © Rick Gayle Studio/CORBIS; t. © Corbis; 49: © Warner Brothers.

Printed in China

07 08 09 XX 9 8 7 6 5 4 3 2 1

ISBN 1-59336-853-4

Design by Witz End Design

Contents

Introduction

You're in advertising already. You're at the center of the advertising business every day. That's because you're able to buy, or influence others to buy, the products that advertising tries to sell. And advertising has become incredibly creative in finding new ways to reach you.

You see advertising on television, of course. You hear it on the radio. You see it along the highway and on the Internet. But you'll also find advertising in places where you might not recognize it. Enter the word *candy* in a computer search engine, and you'll find brands of candy and places that sell them. That's no accident; companies pay for those positions. If, while you're playing a video game, you drive past a road sign with a real brand name on it, chances are good that it was paid for by an advertiser, too. It's not there just to make the game seem more seem realistic!

Notice the logo on the sneakers worn by your favorite basketball player? Of course, it's an ad. It's a big business, creating all these ads. And you're a big part of it, because you're a potential customer. How does it work? How does it affect you? Come find out!

Chapter One

Going Behind the Ads

An advertiser is a company with products or services to sell. An advertising agency is a company that creates the ads that help sell the products or services. The media is the place where the ads appear, such as television or magazines. Advertising is created by a combination of companies and people working together to create messages that attract your attention and, hopefully, convince you to. . . buy. It's one of the most interesting and exciting businesses you can imagine because it combines art, writing, and business like no other industry. I think it's the funnest business in the world!

Advertising is carefully crafted to reach specific people, at specific times, for specific reasons. It's not just flung out in some random way. It's carefully targeted by what the message says, by the pictures it shows, and through the media in which it appears.

In the shows you watch or on the websites you visit, you're seeing things that you're able to buy, or influence your parents to buy for you—sneakers, cereal, toys. An ad targeted toward your parents would look very different from one intended for you. You might see a car advertisement on television, but the car companies don't *intentionally* try to reach you because you're not yet able to drive, and you probably don't have a whole lot to say about which brand of car your family will buy. Television, newspapers, magazines, and outdoor billboards are called mass media because they reach a lot of people at once, including some who aren't really in the target group.

Superbowl, Super Price!

The Superbowl reaches more than 100 million people on Super Sunday. Advertising costs more than $2 million for a 30-second slot. Advertisers know that you and your parents are probably sitting in the same room, watching the same broadcast. That's why they might place an ad for a certain amusement park during the Superbowl broadcast. Your parents can pay for the vacation, and you can influence them to take you, right? That's why the ad is there!

Some Average Rates for 30 Seconds of TV Advertising	
Superbowl	$2.5 million
Friends (final episode)	$2 million
American Idol	$ 700,000
Everybody Hates Chris	$ 179,000
Average Fall 2005	$ 150,000

The Internet Zeroes In Even More

The Internet lets you choose where you want to go, and it also knows a lot about you. It's a one-on-one medium—just you and the computer. When you see a Web banner (that's the little strip ad at the top or side of the Web page) you're being singled out as an individual. You've heard of cookies, right? No, not the kind you eat. On the Internet, cookies are little electronic footprints that track and remember the sites you visit. The Internet probably knows what you've looked at before, maybe even whether you're a boy or a girl, what sorts of toys and sports you like, even the town you live in. Based on information like this, an ad can be selected for your very own tastes and placed right before your eyes.

On Saturday morning television, you might see an ad for a brand of soccer shoe. But on the Internet an ad can tell you where to get the shoe, how much it costs, whether it comes in your favorite color, that your favorite player wears it, and more. The Internet can offer you the life story of that player, a map to the store, and a look at the commercial for the shoe that's running on television. Plus you can send an e-mail to the shoemaker and ask questions. The Internet is a lot more targeted—and a lot more personal—than a mass medium such as television.

You're Bombarded by Advertising!

A funny thing happens when you're surrounded by advertising. You stop noticing it. The constant bombardment of ads means that advertising agencies need to find clever ways to break through the clutter and get your attention. That's where advertising's creative geniuses come in. Creativity in advertising has advanced rapidly over the years because so many ads are competing for your attention. Look at me! Look over here! Listen to this! Pretty soon it's a blur to you, and you may just tune it out.

The Creative Revolution

Most early advertising now seems a little corny and basic. There was a lot less competition for your attention, so proclaiming simple benefits was often enough to make people notice. But as the number of products for sale grew, advertising claims all began to sound alike. Just offering "more cleaning power" would no longer set your soap apart, so advertisers, and their advertising agencies, had to get more creative. The intent was to go beyond proclaiming simple benefits and to make people *feel* good about choosing certain products. Ad agencies wanted people to feel as if a brand could be a friend. The theory was, and still is, that people who have an emotional bond with a product will stay loyal to it. Ask your parents if they prefer a particular brand of laundry detergent, toothpaste, or car. If they do, they're brand loyal.

What's a Benefit?

A product benefit is the thing that makes it superior to a competing brand. It might be a specific fact. A cell phone with a camera has a real benefit over one that doesn't. But when other cell phones all include cameras, they all have to find better benefits to set them apart. A camera phone that "costs less." A "more powerful lens." One that's "easier to operate." These are all product benefits intended to set each brand apart.

As you can see, it's an escalating battle, each brand trying to outdo the other. That's another reason why many advertisers combine facts with feelings. Admiring a brand, feeling that it's "yours," means customers are more loyal and less likely to be swayed when a competitor comes up with a new benefit. At least that's the theory. Think about it in your own life. Do you feel loyal to certain brands of clothes, toys, and foods? Influencing the way you feel is what advertising agencies try to do. If they can affect how you feel, then they might be able to put that feeling into action: You might choose to buy their product over another. And that's what makes the advertising world go 'round.

Don't I Know You?...

Advertising agencies sometimes create characters to represent brands. The power of these images can last for decades. You know these characters. Your parents grew up with them, too. The Pillsbury® Doughboy has been around for over 40 years! The popular Kraft® *Kool-Aid* man appeared first in 1975.

Chapter Two

Going Inside an Advertising Agency

An advertising agency hums like a beehive, powered by interesting, talented people working to create fresh ideas. There are all kinds of roles that support this process. Here are some of the key types of jobs.

1. The Creative Team

The creative people are responsible for finding new ways to express a client's strategy or message. Writers write the words—the headlines for print ads in newspapers and magazines, the scripts for television, the online ads. They're people who have a gift and a love for words and ideas. They like to read.

Writers often team up with art directors. Art directors are the artistic side of the team. They work with photographers to shoot pictures for ads and with film directors to film the television commercials. Art directors have a gift for design, shapes, and colors. Many went to art school. Art directors literally "direct the art." They help coordinate the efforts of a lot of other artistic and creative people in the agency.

Graphic designers create logos and package designs. Studio artists work with art directors to choose typefaces and create different layouts on computers. Some artists draw all day long. They illustrate the storyboards that depict what a television commercial will look like.

Setting the Mood

Every typeface has a name. Some styles of lettering are based on designs that are hundreds of years old. Each style of lettering conveys a different meaning or feeling—serious, fun, light, heavy.

SURFS UP

Good Dog

Garamond

Shelley Script

Helvetica

Haven't I Seen You Somewhere Before?...

Logos identify brands, and must kept up-to-date and fresh.
They're valuable assets recognized by people around the world.

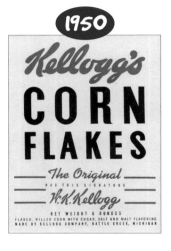

1950

1954

2006

Creative people seldom have to wear conservative business clothes, like suits and ties. They're assumed to be, well, creative—so they get to dress that way. Still, they're skilled at coming up with new ideas and meeting deadlines. It can be tough to be in the creative department. Sometimes a creative person must come up with dozens of ideas before the client selects one.

2. Account Management

Account managers are the people who run the business part of the advertising account. They develop a relationship with the client. Some advertising clients spend hundreds of millions of dollars. It takes a skilled person, good with numbers and organizing, to keep track of all that. The account managers develop schedules that everyone in the agency needs to follow. Every ad has a deadline—a specific time when it has to reach the television network or go up on the Internet. It can't be late because the time and space have already been paid for. Does that sound like a lot of pressure? It is!

The nickname for the account managers is "suits." That's because in the early days, many of them dressed more conservatively, in suits and ties, when they met with their clients. Often they still do. They're the business engines of the agency.

3. Research

Researchers (or planners) interview customers and compile data that helps agencies understand what kind of advertising messages might work best. Advertising messages aren't just lucky guesses. Not ever! They're based on customer opinions, careful planning, and a lot of statistical data.

Researchers also track the success (or failure) of the advertising campaign. It's important to know how an ad is doing, in case you need to alter it to make it work better. Researchers are good thinkers. Some come from backgrounds such as mathematics and statistics. They're good with numbers. A lot of researchers also come from areas such as psychology, or even anthropology. They're people who know what makes other people tick. They're curious to find better ways to reach customers with the right advertising message.

4. Production

The production department gets advertising materials ready to go to the media. Television commercials must be filmed, radio scripts recorded, and ad layouts prepared for newspapers, magazines, and online. Take two newspapers and place them side by side. Notice their size differences? The production people have to create dozens of differently sized ads for all different sizes of publications. Sometimes that can mean doing the same print ad in hundreds of sizes! And before any ads go to the media, they have to be checked by the creative and account people responsible for them. Many agencies even have a separate department, the traffic department, just to be sure the right ads get to the right people and places.

Measure Twice, Cut Once!

Newspapers and magazines are different sizes. The production department makes sure the right sizes are created and reach the publications in time for printing. It can be a very complex process.

A Sampling of Magazine and Newspaper Trim Sizes in Inches	
TIME Magazine	7.875 x 10.5
Teen People	8.25 x 10.75
Bon Appetit	8 3/8 x 10 13/16
The Washington Post Magazine	8 x 10 1/2
The New York Times	13 x 21

Lights, Camera, Action!

The average cost to produce a television commercial in the United States is $350,000. That doesn't include the cost of running it on television. That's just the price to shoot and edit it. Some commercials cost millions to shoot. For that reason every detail in product presentation is carefully analyzed and crafted to perfection.

Television producers help manage the complicated process of filming a TV commercial. A single TV commercial can cost a million dollars or more, and involve hundreds of people and dozens of locations. Agency producers work with special effects companies to create graphics for commercials, and with musicians and recording studios to create the soundtracks. People in production are plugged into the world of music, film, and graphic arts. They're good at organizing people and schedules, and managing budgets. Like most people in advertising, they are multi-talented. Does it all sound exciting and interesting? Well, it is!

Whenever you see someone behind the wheel in a car commercial, it's usually been shot with the car on a trailer, towed by a camera truck. The car is pulled along the road, and the driver pretends to steer. This lets the driver concentrate on his or her role without having to act and drive at the same time! As you can see, the trailer that the car sits on also forms a platform for lighting the driver. This keeps the light on his or her face consistent and even, even if the weather turns cloudy or the car goes into a shady spot on the road.

Chapter Three

An Ad Campaign Starts With You

The advertising game begins with you, the consumer. Advertising is intended to reach you directly because you have the power to buy. Or maybe it's directed at you because you're an "influencer" with the power to beg an adult to take you to a particular movie, amusement park, or buy a certain video game or cereal. To show you how advertising gets created, let's pick something really basic and create an advertising campaign for it. As you'll see, there's a lot more to it than just making a clever TV commercial.

The ACME Gum Corp.

Let's say you like chewing gum. Doesn't everybody?

The chief of marketing at ACME Gum Corporation (we're making this up) needs to increase sales. ACME currently makes two kinds of gumballs: grape and orange, sold in separate packages of five. The marketing director thinks ACME can sell more gum if they combine grape and orange in the same pack. So the marketing director at ACME talks to the account manager at the advertising agency. Hmm. Let's call it Olson, Wilkerson & Worley Advertising. OWW! for short. Does the account manager at OWW! call in the creative team to make an ad? Not yet. First, he calls in Rona Worley, the head of research at OWW!.

What's in a Name?

Many ad agencies are named for the people who started them. When a long string of names gets too cumbersome, agencies are referred to by the first letters of the founders' names. JWT, one of the world's largest agencies, stands for J. Walter Thompson, which was founded in 1864.

Leo Burnett

DDB

JWT

Ogilvy

Rona the Researcher

Research? Now? Wahhhh! Can't we just go do something clever and fun? Not yet. Rona first has to find out if the customer (you!) cares about having two flavors of gum in one package. No need to spend money to make a bunch of ads if the idea has no appeal. No need to go to all the trouble of packing orange and grape gumballs, then shipping them to stores everywhere, if nobody cares, right? Rona's job is to find out if anybody cares.

So she does a couple of things. She sets up focus groups for people like you. Focus groups are small clusters of six to eight consumers who are brought together by advertising agencies to explore ideas and ads before they're taken into production.

Rona the researcher also investigates the validity of the new gum idea by going into online chat rooms and asking if anyone would be interested in having orange and grape gum sold in the same package. (Okay, maybe a lot of people don't chat about gum online, but a few might. You get the idea. Also, it's good to realize that chat rooms are excellent places for marketers to gather customer information.) In addition, Rona might actually set up online focus groups to find out if the idea has appeal. Here's what she learns.

Eddie, who's 12 and lives in Lubbock, Texas, attends a focus group and thinks mixing the flavors is a swell idea. He's already a fan of ACME's Orange Squeeze gum, and he likes Grape Gonzo, too. A lot of boys in the research group voice similar opinions. Raoul, in Sacramento, California, says he likes "the choice of having both flavors in one pack."

Susan, who's 10 and lives in Queens, New York, has a different opinion. She thinks the idea is sort of boring. "Big deal," she says in an online focus group. "Just putting them together in one pack doesn't do a lot for me. What else you got?" Erika, in Miami, Florida, says she buys gum because she likes to blow bubbles. "Having two flavors in one pack would be okay, but I really want bigger bubbles."

"Hmmm," says Rona the researcher. "This could get interesting."

Meanwhile, Back at the Ad Ranch

Rona holds a meeting with the client from ACME and the agency's account manager. "It seems from the research," she says, "that our target audience of boys likes having grape and orange in the same pack, but the girls are less than blown away by it." Everyone groans. Matching the right product with the right message for the right people is the challenge of every advertising agency. It's complicated because the audience (you!) are complex and varied. "If we could offer the choice of flavors in one pack, and find a way to make bigger bubbles, too, then we might have something that appeals to both boys and girls."

The room falls silent. "We have the technology to make bigger bubbles," says the client. "We can add a special elastomer to the gum mix."

"Let's go for it," says Rona. "Orange and grape gum in the same pack, with more bubble power!" What happens next? Well, they all go to lunch, of course. After lunch the next stop is the creative department, where ace copywriter Ryan Wright and art director extraordinaire Penny Escobar are ready to roll.

You Gotta Have a Name!

Ryan the writer studied advertising and English in college. Someday he wants to write a book. Art director Penny Escobar paints late at night in her apartment, where she lives with her cat, Ed. Ryan and Penny team up. They know the new product from ACME will be orange and grape gum combined in one package with better bubble power. But there's one thing they need before they can create an ad campaign. They need a name!

"How about GOB?" says Ryan.

"What?" says Penny. "That's crazy!"

Celebrity Impostors

Some product names are so distinctive that they are sometimes used to describe an entire category of products. Companies work hard to prevent their product names from becoming "generic" like that. They don't want their distinctive names to be lost in the shuffle of brands. It might sound weird, but the correct way to refer to some of these familiar products is "a box of Kleenex™ brand tissues" or "Jello™ brand gelatin dessert."

"No, listen. It stands for grape, orange, bubbles."

"Okay, if you say so," says Penny. "But it sounds like a gob of gum or something."

"I know. That's why I like it."

"Gross," says Penny.

"Chews GOB," says Ryan. "See, *chews* sounds like *choose*."

"Clever. But still gross," Penny says. She leans back in her chair and kicks off her shoes (creative people get to do this sort of thing).

"Wayva Flayva," says Penny.

"That's cool," says Ryan. "It's a wave of flavor. A different one each time."

The account manager pops his head in. "How about Smacko?"

"I get it," says Penny. "Like the flavors smack you in the mouth?"

"Right," says the account manager. "And the big bubble does, too, when it pops!"

"It's on the list," says Ryan the writer.

Advertising is fun because it's collaborative. People work together to frame ideas, and everyone's thoughts are welcome.

Penny has asked Artie Foxx, a graphic designer in the agency's studio, to illustrate how the three names might look on packages. He's created three package versions with the three possible names: GOB, Wayva Flayva, and Smacko. Ad agencies do a lot of this kind of simulation before the actual package or ad exists. These examples are called comps. That's short for *composite*, meaning a rough composition of elements that simulate how an ad or package might look. In an agency, people spend a lot of time "comping up" packages and ads, so that everyone involved in the process can envision the idea and offer an opinion. It's hard work, but every day you're creating something new.

You Want to Call It What?!

These are some of the names that didn't make the final list. What names can you think up for ACME's orange and grape gum?

Chooza!

GRAPO!

TWOFER BLOFER!

BORANGE

ComboBongo

The Client Calls the Names

The client at ACME likes the names. Well, one of them anyway.

"I'm not so sure about Wayva Flayva," says the client.

Ryan the writer responds, "It's supposed to mean that you taste orange, then you can taste another wave of flavor with grape."

But the client isn't swayed. "Flavor is important, but what's the key message we really need to communicate here?"

"I believe it's about choice," remarks Rona. "Now you can choose the flavor you want from a single pack, and you can choose to get bigger bubbles."

"Exactly," says the client. "Wayva Flayva is clever, but I'm not sure it's really saying the right things about the product."

So Wayva Flayva is out. Down in flames. That's the way it goes in advertising. You create a lot of ideas; you also throw away a lot of ideas.

Smacko Gets Spanked

"Smacko sounds a little violent to me," the client continues. "Do we think kids will like the idea of getting conked in the head by a gumball, or having bubbles pop all over their faces?" (These are the kinds of questions clients ask. They're very protective of the ideas that represent their brands.)

"Yes!" says Ryan the writer. "Guys love crazy stuff like that!" A hush falls over the room, like a fog.

"Uh, we wondered the same thing," says Penny, looking at her feet. "Girls like the bubble aspect of the product, but..."

Rona jumps in, "...we're not sure they'll like the idea of gum popping in their hair."

"All right," says Ryan. "I can see I'm outnumbered."

"GOB seems really clever," the client says. " It's memorable, because the letters represent the product idea: grape, orange, bubbles. G-O-B."

"It could be so cool," says Ryan.

"Maybe," says Penny. "It just can't be gross."

"GOB definitely helps communicate the choice between two flavors in one pack, with bigger bubbles," reminded Rona.

"Right," says the client. "Let's not forget our central strategy here. Customers get to choose."

The room falls silent. The answer is right in front of them.

"GOB," says the client.

"GOB it is!" cheers the agency team.

"See you in two weeks," says the account manager.

The cheering stops. The good news is that the agency now has a clear direction. The bad news is that they have a deadline—two weeks away. That's the way it goes in the ad business. You always have deadlines. How do you think they'll do?

"Right. See you in two weeks," says the client.

Gobs of Ideas Get Pitched

The moment of truth arrives two weeks later. The client comes to the advertising agency office to see the ad campaign for GOB. This is called a "pitch," like a "sales pitch." You throw out some ideas, and you hope the client will like them. And that's just what Ryan, Penny, Rona, and the account manager will do today.

They start with the television commercial. A TV commercial is often, but not always, the centerpiece of an ad campaign. A TV commercial uses sight and sound to express an idea. It's a lively and fun place around which a lot of other elements can fit.

"The strategic idea is that GOB gives kids a choice," reminds Rona the researcher. "Kids live in a world where choices are usually made by adults. In a small way, GOB gives kids control. They can choose grape, orange, bubbles."

Penny picks up the pitch. "Imagine if kids got to make other choices that they dream about."

"So, gum is a dream come true?" says the client. "Isn't that a little over the top?"

"Yes," says the account manager, "but that's what makes it fun."

"And," adds Ryan, "since bubbles figure into it and are sort of balloon-like, and balloons float, we figured that the ultimate dream for kids could be ..."

"What?" says the client, pounding the table. "What's the ultimate dream for kids?"

This is exactly what Ryan and Penny had hoped for. The client is fired up to hear their dramatic idea.

"The ultimate dream of kids is to fly," says Penny.

"Research backs it up," says Rona the researcher. "Kids want to chew gum, blow bubbles, and fly. Mary Poppins flew. Harry Potter flew. Superman flew. It's part of kid culture." Rona knows her stuff.

The Idea Seems to be Flying

"How are you going to get real kids to fly?" says the client. "Isn't there an insurance issue with that? Or are we going to just tie strings on them and hang them out of airplanes while we film?"

"No, no," says the account manager. "We'll use green screen."

"What's that?" says the client. "Can we afford it?"

"We'll explain it later," says the account manager.

"So," continues Ryan, "we've got GOB-chewing kids flying along, and they're saying this stupid rhyme."

"Stupid?" asks the client.

"Goofy," says Penny reassuringly. "It's goofy. Not stupid."

Ryan continues. "It's a limerick, sort of. And they're chewing GOB the whole time. Their mouths are full of gobs of GOB. So it looks really funny. It's very memorable."

"Okay. If you say so," says the client. He is not convinced.

Penny soldiers on. "The campaign is focused on an ordinary kid with an ordinary name—Bob. And when he chews GOB, his dreams come true; he gets to fly. And so do his friends," says Penny.

"Show me the storyboards," says the client.

The Storyboard Sails Out of the Bag

At this stage the advertising agency is asking the client to take a risk and approve something he can't even see that will cost him thousands of dollars. There's no television commercial in front of him yet, because it hasn't been filmed. So how do advertising agencies get clients to take this leap of faith? They use a storyboard—a series of hand-drawn pictures that look sort of like cartoons. A storyboard shows the images that will be filmed later. It helps everyone visualize the progression of a television spot. In the end, though, it won't be a cartoon. It will be filmed to look real.

Ryan points to the first frame of the storyboard. "Okay, a boy flying over his neighborhood, looking down at all his pals, mouth full of GOB, says, 'I'm Bob, part of the mob that chews GOB!' And the boys on the ground looking up say, 'We're the mob mentioned by Bob that chews GOB!' And the boys blow huge bubbles that lift them into the air. Some have orange bubbles, and some have grape. So now all these boys are flying along, blowing bubbles alongside Bob."

Ryan is on the third frame now, leading the client through the storyboard. Penny picks up here. "Then we see girls standing in the treetops, like birds. Some blow grape bubbles and some orange-colored bubbles. A girl says, 'Hey, Bob, us girls are a mob that chews GOB!' Then the girls hop off their branches and join Bob and the boys flying along. So now there are hundreds of kids in the sky. And Bob says, 'Choose dreams over troubles; grape, orange and bubbles; come fly with the mob that chews GOB!'"

There's Just One thing Missing

The client smiles. "It's very clever," he says. "But where's my product?"

Clients say this a lot. They're always interested in getting more shots and mentions of their product in the advertising. This is understandable, but many creative people in advertising agencies think that putting too much product in a commercial takes the fun out of it. It just makes it so "commercial" that people roll their eyes and don't care. There is some truth to both sides of this argument. The next time you watch television, see if you can count all the product shots and mentions. Sometimes you'll see a lot, and sometimes you'll see more of a funny story being told without so much product. But Ryan the writer and Penny the art director are clever, creative people. They know they aren't making art here. It's a commercial—it's meant to sell something.

Ryan carries on. "Then we cut to a pack shot (a close-up shot of the package is called a 'pack shot' in advertising-ese) of a GOB package with Bob's face beside it. And a voice-over (an announcer, in other words) in a big, deep voice says, 'Join the Mob. Chews GOB!'"

"I see," says the client. "You're doing a word play with *chews* and *choose*. That's clever. But shouldn't it be a mob that *chew* GOB? I'm not sure your grammar is correct there."

"You're right," says Rona the researcher. "It's pretty bad English, but we want to reinforce the wordplay on *chews* and *choose*.

In advertising, you have permission to butcher the English language sometimes to suit your purposes. Wordplays are common. Using either homophones or words with double meanings can be a fun way of communicating two messages at once, such as *chews*, which is what you do with gum, and *choose*, which sounds the same.

The Plot Extends So Much Further

"I like it," says the client. "What else you got?" The TV ad is just the starting point for the creative campaign.

"Well, since we're showing kids flying, we thought we'd paint an airplane with the GOB colors, and call it AIR GOB ONE, " says the account manager.

Something like a painted airplane is called a "promotion." Contests and prizes are promotions. They're a different form of advertising, but they're still ads.

"An airplane?" glares the client. "How many billions of dollars will I need for that?"

"It's actually quite feasible," says the account manager. "We lease the plane and paint it. Then we have a contest, and the winners get to bring their families on a trip."

"A trip to . . ." The client seems concerned.

"To meet Bob, at his house in Orlando," says Penny.

"Bob has a house in Orlando?" asks the client. "I thought Bob was just a made-up character who led the GOB mob—or whatever you're calling it."

"We'll build a house—a pretend mansion—at an amusement park in Orlando," says Ryan enthusiastically. He whips out a drawing of Bob's house. "So we can bring kids to the park! And one of the things they can do is hang with Bob at the..."

"Don't tell me. Let me guess," says the client. "...with Bob at the House of GOB."

"Actually," says Ryan the writer, "it's House o' GOB, not House of GOB. It just sounds cooler like that."

"Of course," says the client. "I knew that."

"We knew you knew," says the account manager.

Getting in the Game Online

"Okay," says the client. "But what's the contest? What do kids have to do to win the trip to Bob's House o' GOB?"

"You're gonna love this," says the account manager.

"I'll be the judge of that," says the client.

"Okay," says Penny, "the contest is an online video game. A competition between GOB chewers. The top 50 winners get the trip!"

"What's the game?" says the client.

"It's simple," says Ryan. "Bob is in his house with his family. If he can blow a big enough GOB bubble, he can float away and fly with his mob. There's just one problem. Bob's little sister is jealous and wants to pop the bubble."

"So," adds Penny, "you have to put down a force field that shields Bob's bubble from his little sister."

"And I suppose she's running after him with blunt scissors, correct?" asks the client.

"No, no scissors! Not a good idea," says Penny. "She'll have a pushpin."

"Right," says Ryan. "And when she gets near Bob, you drop a force field in front of her so she conks into it and falls down."

The client lays his head on the table and moans. "We're going to get letters from parents on this," he wails.

Dream Job!

Online gaming is a growing medium for advertisers, especially those who want to reach kids. A lot of the games you see online aren't just created by crazy gamers locked in their basements cooking up cool games. They're created by crazy gamers who are paid by advertisers and ad agencies to come up with cool games. Believe it or not, you can actually get a job making and playing video games.

"Don't worry," says the account manager, patting the client on the back. "The kid's okay. She's fine, really. We'll have our public relations group draft a response that says it's all just a joke."

This does not seem to help the client feel better.

The account manager continues. "We'll also have our PR team draft some remarks for the news cameras if the television stations show up at ACME headquarters..."

The client wails even louder. "Oh, great!"

"It's a breakthrough idea," says Penny.

"Cutting edge!" says Ryan.

"Impossible to forget!" says Rona the researcher. Rona will be in charge of tracking the campaign after it runs.

It's been a long morning. Time for a break. The meeting is adjourned for lunch. Ryan and Penny go outside to the basketball court. The account manager and the client go to the pool table. What? An office equipped with stuff like that? Sure! A lot of advertising agencies have fun equipment around to help the staff blow off steam. Some even have "creative rooms" with pillows on the floor to help people relax and come up with ideas.

Will the Pitch Be a Hit?

The meeting resumes. Everyone sits quietly around the conference room table. Some are looking at their shoes. Some stare out the window. The client speaks. "First of all, thank you for your amazing efforts today. You've shown me some very challenging, creative ideas." He looks at Ryan and Penny. "In fact, some of them scare me to death. But I believe it's time for ACME to take a risk and try something different."

Everyone is looking at the client. "Let's do it," he says.

"Which parts of the campaign, specifically, would you like to do?" asks the account manager.

"All of it," says the client.

Rarely do you hear this from a client. Many times there are long discussions and lists of tiny changes that, over time, wear everyone down and often result in ads that aren't as good as they might have been. But this time a miracle has occurred, and the client has approved it all.

Yaaay! The Deadline Looms!

"Hooray," say Penny and Ryan, high-fiving.

"All right!" say Rona and the account manager, hugging and dancing around the room, tears streaming down their faces. Advertising people can be very passionate about what they do. They're really creating something, and that something has special meaning for them. But after a few minutes of glee, the room falls silent.

"We have a lot of work to do," whispers Penny.

"Oh, yeah. Now we have actually have to go *do* all this stuff," says Ryan.

"That's right," says the client. "And the deadline is a month away."

Once again the moment of celebration is short.

Ryan picks up his coat and heads for the door. "See you tomorrow, Penny," he says.

"Okay, see you mañana," she says.

At home, Penny finds Ed asleep on the window seat. "Wake up, Ed," she says. "We've got work to do." Ed looks at her. His ideas are limited to eating. But he loves Penny and sits on her lap to help her think. He's not a big-idea cat. He's just a cat.

Chapter Four

Fun and Games (mostly)

Thinking up an ad campaign takes one set of skills. But bringing it to life takes different talents and people. This is where the agency's broadcast production department starts rolling.

The Producers Start Producing

Pam is the agency producer in charge of getting the commercial made. It's a complex job—scheduling all the people who will cast and shoot the commercial, and handling the finances of a project that can cost a million dollars or more.

First, they have to find their spokeskid, Bob. Bob isn't some fellow actually named Bob who flies, of course—he's an actor. And most actors are found by casting agents, who bring in dozens of kids and ask them to "read for the part." In this case the kids trying out for the Bob character will be asked to read a line from the commercial: "I'm Bob, part of the mob that chews GOB."

But there are thousands of young actors out there. So Penny and Ryan have to specify the kind of person they think will typify Bob. Here are their specs.

Casting About for Bob

The casting agent puts out the word, and dozens of kids attend the session, accompanied by a parent. These kids are actors who are trying to break into the business. Appearing in commercials is a good way to be seen by directors and people in the entertainment business. Some of the most famous actors in Hollywood, such as John Travolta, Brooke Shields, and Lindsay Lohan, started this way.

Penny and Ryan narrow their choice to one boy—Harold Hubbard. He has a certain "Bob-like" quality that seems right. He's fun, and he seems genuinely nice. He's the kind of kid others would like to follow. He's a good actor, reading his lines convincingly. There's just one problem—he has long brown hair and doesn't wear glasses.

The glasses are no big deal. The agency will simply make up some glasses with clear lenses for him to wear. But what about the hair? The casting agent discusses it with Harold and his mom, who quickly agree that coloring and cutting Harold's hair will not be a problem. It will grow back.

So there you go. An instant blond. A kid with perfectly good eyesight wearing glasses. A boy named Harold who suddenly becomes the perfect "Bob." In advertising it happens all the time.

Specs for Bob

10 years old
Good-natured, not spoiled
Mischievious, not mean
A twinkle of fun in his eyes
A leader
Short blond hair
Freckles
Glasses

Dealing With the Director, Deleon

Penny and Ryan, in collaboration with Pam the producer, have selected Deleon to direct their television commercial. What is Deleon's last name, you ask? Well, he doesn't have one. In fact, his real name is Lou Melvin. It's not unheard of for directors and high-profile creative types to assume a single, dramatic name. Deleon says his name was given to him by a shaman in the jungle, and that it harkens back to Juan Ponce de León, the explorer who discovered Florida. Deleon says the shaman told him that he is a "visual explorer." Whatever.

It's probably a good name, because Deleon will have the very challenging task of exploring a highly visual little filmlet (a commercial is 30 seconds of film) where hundreds of kids are flying, blowing bubbles, and saying goofy rhymes, all at the same time.

Hundreds of hours, and hundreds of thousands of dollars, will go into this 30 seconds. As people in the advertising business say, making a television commercial is like "painting the Sistine Chapel on the head of pin." It's a lot of visual perfection in a very small space. But portraying products at their very best is often well worth the money, because how a product is perceived in its advertising can make all the difference.

But first, Penny and Ryan must shift gears from the TV commercial to the online gaming component of the GOB campaign. Being a creative person in an advertising agency means being able to work in variety of media while facing multiple deadlines.

A Game Is Really a Story

Creating an online game is sort of like sketching out the storyline of a movie. You have to create the characters, define how they behave, and figure out the progression of the story.

"So what do we call it?" Penny wonders.

"How about 'Bob Gets GOB'?" says Ryan.

"We have to get the house in. The prize to the top 50 players is to go visit Bob's house in Orlando," Penny reminds him.

"Okay, how about 'Bob's House o' GOB'?"

"Sure, why not? 'Bob's House o' GOB' it is," she writes. "Who's inside the house?"

"Well," muses Ryan, "there's Bob, of course. And his little sister. His mom or dad. Maybe some others. What happens?"

"I'd say that Bob's chewing GOB, and when the bubble gets big enough, he floats out of the house and joins his mob flying in the sky."

Just then there's a knock at the door. It's Ernie the engineer, the agency's gaming expert. He'll help design the software that makes the game work.

"Whassup, dudes?" says Ernie the engineer. Ernie has a ponytail and a beard. He wears cut-offs and says *dude* a lot.

"I'm not a dude, Ernie," says Penny.

"You are *so not* a dude. You're a dudette," grins Ernie. Penny likes Ernie because Ernie likes cats. "So you got this Bob guy in the house trying to blow a GOB bubble so he can fly away with his dudes, but his sister wants to pop it?"

"You got it," says Ryan.

"Cool," says Ernie. "Sis can come from any direction, right? Runnin' straight at the dude's bubble with a pushpin?"

"Yep, that's the way we see it," says Penny.

"So what if you drop a force field, what happens?" Ernie asks.

"Little sister conks into the shield and disappears for ten seconds," says Ryan, "which buys you nearly enough time to pump up the bubble and float away."

"Then she comes back, like from a different room, maybe with her annoying dog, on the attack again," says Ernie. "And we'll have different levels, like when you fly away three times, or you catch Little Sis three times, you go upstairs to a different room. And more people start coming in. Like there's Mom or Dad coming faster and faster, and maybe Grandma with a knitting needle. Or maybe Bob's cat with really sharp claws. He's like sort of a crazy cat. Not well-behaved, like Ed." He grinned at Penny.

"Cooool!" say Penny and Ryan together. Ernie knows his stuff.

Can you believe this is a real job?

Ernie rolls on. "Tap the space bar to blow up the bubble. Tap the arrow keys to place the force fields in front of the people who want to pop it. And we should, like, do a full body-shield button that gives you three free puffs on the GOB bubble."

"Right, but you get only three full body shields," says Penny.

"Yeah, and whenever Bob gets his bubble popped, he has to open the GOB pack and put another piece in his mouth," adds Ryan. "And since there are five GOBs to a pack, when Bob runs out of gum, the game is over."

Cool!

Okay, It's Not All Just Fun and Games

Just then the account manager wanders by and adds, "And we get to see a great big GOB logo *every time* he has to reload his gum, right?"

"Oh, yeah!" says Ernie. "We got to sell gum here, my man."

"I love it when you say that, Ernie," says the account manager.

"Okay, chill, dude. I'm hanging with my dudes here." The account manager knows it's time to move on.

"So how do we score this puppy?" asks Ernie. "What if you get 1,000 points for every force field that stops Little Sis? Then you get 10,000 points when you get the bubble big enough to fly."

"And you high-five one of the mob that's flying overhead," says Penny.

"And the highest level puts Bob up on the roof! And there's Little Sis, and Mom or Dad, and Granny and the crazy cat, and a wacko gardener with a shovel and..." Ryan stops to take a breath.

"This so rocks!" says Ernie. "Let me go. My dudes can so deal with this."

Ernie's dudes? He means his colleagues in the development studio. Once the game is outlined, it takes a lot of computer wizards to animate it and make all the actions happen. The simplest games can take months to create. The really complex ones, such as the ones you play at home, can take years! Game designers like Ernie and his dudes are an important part of the advertising campaign. Can you imagine getting paid to spend all day creating video games? Lots of people do!

Chapter Five

Bringing Bob (and GOB) to Life

It's time to shoot the TV ad. But it won't be shot "on location" in a neighborhood with Bob flying overhead looking down at the houses and the other kids. It will be shot on a sound stage—a giant building about the size of an airplane hangar made especially for shooting movies and commercials. There's room to build an entire town inside! It's called a sound stage because it's insulated from outside noises, so the sounds of airplanes and sirens won't interfere with the recording of the actors' voices.

Los Angeles, or Hollywood, is the capital of commercial production and has many stages, studios, and services that support the movie and commercial industry. Many commercials are shot on stages in New York City, too. But a commercial can be shot on location as well. When that happens, the crews and cameras are trucked to the location and spend several days, or even weeks, shooting a movie outside or in real houses and buildings "on location."

Making It Up vs. Making It Real

So why not shoot the GOB spot outside, in a real neighborhood? First of all, hanging hundreds of kids in the air over a house is not very safe. Nobody would permit that. But shooting outside also means that the light is constantly changing as the sun moves, or clouds block it, creating shadows. Film needs a consistent, controllable light source in order to look right. And sometimes it's cold outside or it rains. Having hundreds of children and crew standing in the rain is not a good idea. That's why Deleon the director has chosen a technique called "green screen" (sometimes called blue screen) instead. Against a giant green screen, you can create reality that's actually better than the real thing!

The Day No Kids Would Fly

When Penny and Ryan walk onto the sound stage, they see a huge wall, 100 feet long and 50 feet high, painted bright green. They look at each other, incredulous. "Where are the houses Bob's flying over?" they ask.

"Right here," says Deleon. He points them to a TV monitor where they see film of rooftops and an empty sky. The camera moves slowly from left to right as if it's tracking something in the air. But there's nothing there... yet. It's just empty sky above the rooftops. "Today we'll shoot the kids flying against green screen," says Deleon. "Then we'll insert them into this film of the sky. You'll never know they aren't really flying!"

"Okay, hook 'em up!" yells Deleon to the film crew. Ten boys and ten girls are positioned a few feet off the floor, in harnesses. They're dangling in front of the giant green screen. "Okay, act like you're flying when I say 'Action!'" he yells. "Ready...and action!" (Directors still say "action" to tell the actors when to start "acting," and yell "cut" when they want them to stop. *Cut* is short for "cut off the cameras." But you knew that.)

It's All About Turning Green to Blue

What is going on here? Twenty boys and girls are flapping their arms, dangling in harnesses three feet off the floor (there are pads on the floor, of course) in front of a giant green screen. But the sky is blue, right? And the kids are supposed to be flying in a blue sky, right? Well, the editor of the commercial will take the film Deleon shot of the blue sky and rooftops and combine it with the film of the kids flapping in front of the green screen. Then he'll drop the color green out from behind the kids and let the blue sky come through. Converting film images into digital formats allows filmmakers to do amazing things. The same techniques are used in commercials.

"Cut!" yells Deleon. All the kids sag in their harnesses. And where are their parents? They're standing right there in the corner, keeping their eyes on their kids. There are also a nurse, a firefighter, and a monitor from a child welfare agency "on set" to make sure everything is done safely. If the shoot interferes with school, the kids may even have a teacher on set to work with them between takes. Safety rules and workplace regulations are very strict when kids appear in commercials. As they should be.

Pucker Up, Kids!

"I forgot something, kids," says Deleon. "You have to pucker your lips and act like you're blowing bubbles. Let's do it again, please."

You thought the kids would actually be blowing their own bubbles? Stop and think about it. Twenty kids are blowing different size bubbles all at once. Some can't get their bubbles going, and some pop too soon. It would be *impossible* to get them all to look the same, so the bubbles will be shot later and added to the film. Deleon will film perfect "master bubbles" in orange and in grape, blown by a professional stylist. (Stylists make food look perfect for the camera. It's a specialized art to make a hamburger look juicy, ice cream look yummy and creamy, and salad look fresh and crisp for the camera.) Then the editor will take this perfect bubble and digitally place it on each kid's puckered-up lips so they'll be uniformly perfect.

"Okay, ready now. Flap your arms like you're flying and pucker your lips like you're blowing bubbles, everyone. And...action!"

It's a weird scene—kids flapping around in harnesses, lips puckered, a giant green screen behind them. But it's pretty ordinary in the world of making commercials. The green screen concept is used to create all sorts of impossible scenes and situations, such as people standing on icebergs or on a planet in outer space.

Ten Kids Become 100

"Cut!" yells Deleon. The kids wiggle out of their harnesses and troop out the door to the wardrobe trailer. The wardrobe stylist (this stylist manages all the clothes and costumes worn by the actors) puts new outfits on some of the kids, and gives some of them glasses and hats so they'll look like totally different characters. The makeup and hair stylists give several of the kids wigs and even apply different noses and different right ears to some of them (they don't need the left ear because it's not facing the camera). They'll return and reshoot the flying scenes in three or four costumes and disguises, so that the editor can make the same 20 kids look like hundreds when he places them all in the sky.

Charlie and the Chocolate Factory

Charlie and the Chocolate Factory is a great example of use of green screens, and of a single actor who plays multiple roles. All of the Oompa-Loompas are played by one fellow.

The Girls Go Climb a Tree. Not Really.

"Cut!" yells Deleon. "Next we'll shoot the girls standing in the tree as Bob flies by. Girls only now!"

The boys take a break, and the girls get ready for their scene. Remember, they're standing in a treetop when Bob flies by, and one girl says, "Hey, Bob, us girls are a mob that chews GOB!"

But where's the tree? Well, it's on film—shot the day before, miles from the sound stage—a beautiful pear tree, whose leaves have turned a lovely deep red for fall. You see, some of the girls' parents might have had a slight problem asking their girls to stand up in the branches of a tree for three hours. But, thanks to Hollywood, there's a better way. The grips (a grip is a stagehand—someone who does the heavy lifting on a commercial shoot) roll a set of green steps in front of the green screen. The girls stand on the steps at all different levels. When this scene is applied over the film of the real tree and the green is erased, it will look as if the girls are standing on the branches.

"Okay," says Deleon, "after Angie says her line," (Angie is the girl with the speaking role) "give a little hop so we can make it look like you're taking off to fly."

The Girls' Mob Hops To It!

"Action!" yells Deleon, standing at the camera. The soundman swings his boom—a long pole with a microphone attached to the end—right over Angie's head as she says, "Hey, Bob! Us girls are a mob that chews GOB!"

"Now, girls, hop!" screams Deleon. The girls do a little hop. Later the editor will cut this shot to the scene shot earlier where the girls are flying in their harnesses in front of the green screen. The magic of editing will make you believe that the girls hopped off the tree and began flying through the air. The little hop action will help you "buy" the edit. If you watch television closely, you'll spot the little tricks that make a 30-second commercial tell a much longer story.

"Cut!" yells Deleon. "Moving on!"

The Star Has His Moment in the Sling

What's left to shoot? Well, our hero, of course. You remember Bob. He's an actor named Harold Hubbard, a fourth grader who really has brown hair, but who now has blond hair and wears glasses that he

doesn't need. Bob is hooked into his harness in front of the trusty green screen. In case you're wondering, the editor will digitally erase the harnesses on all the kids later. You'll never see a wire, just kids who appear to be flying through the air blowing perfect bubbles.

Bob is hoisted up. "Action!" yells Deleon.

"I'm Bob, part of the mob that chews GOB!"

"Cut! Excellent!" says Deleon. But even though the take is excellent, they do it a dozen more times, just to be sure they have it. Bob nails it every time.

"It's a wrap!" yells Deleon. That means the shoot is "in the can." It's an old term that means that they have the shots they need: The film has been taken out of the camera and placed in a film can ready to be developed. Many commercials and movies are still shot on real film, and then transferred to a digital format that can be edited and manipulated into the final commercial.

Meanwhile, the Gum Is Rolling

All this work on the advertising campaign happens at the same time that ACME is ramping up actual production of GOB gum. The gum has to be manufactured, then packaged, then delivered to stores all over the country. The ACME sales team has to go out to stores and negotiate space on the shelves for the new product. The accounting department at ACME has to decide how much the new gum should cost. Should it cost a little more, since you're getting a choice of grape and orange plus bigger bubbles? Or should it be priced the same as regular ACME gum? The client works with his team inside ACME and with the advertising agency to make some of these decisions. But they have to hurry. Launch day is just weeks away, and there's still a lot to do!

The PR Machine Cranks Up

Public Relations, or PR, can also be part of the advertising mix used to sell new products. Paul from the PR division of OWW! Advertising flies to Orlando to supervise the construction of Bob's House o' GOB. Paul has negotiated a deal with a major amusement park to build the house inside the park, where 50 winners of the online game can fly in on AIR GOB ONE (remember the airplane painted in GOB colors with Bob's face on it?) to meet Bob and hang with him for a day. What does the house look like? Well, the actual house being built in Orlando has to look exactly like the house in the online video game, right? Paul checks the house against the design from Ernie in the online design studio. ("It's gotta match, dude!")

This is how advertising takes an idea from the imagination into something real. It brings Bob and his house out of the television set, or the computer, and literally makes them a part of your life. On the day the advertising campaign launches, Paul from PR will hold a press conference here at the house. He'll bring in reporters from television networks and newspapers on AIR GOB ONE and show off the house and arrange interviews with Bob.

PR Turns Advertising Into News

The goal of PR is to get a product mentioned in the press or on television. When that happens, it's like free advertising, and it takes many forms. Some of the photos in magazines, or "news" items you see on television, are actually "photo ops" (short for photo opportunities) or "media events" created by public relations companies for their clients.

When you see a movie star holding a particular model of cell phone or brand of handbag, chances are good that a PR person has given the star that item and encouraged the star to use it or wear it in order to be seen and photographed with it. When the paparazzi take a shot of the star leaving a restaurant, the cell phone or handbag shows up in magazines all over the country, along with the photo of the star. PR is an advertising technique used heavily by the movie and publishing industries. Ever notice that a movie star just happens to appear on a TV talk show and four magazine covers just before his or her movie is released? It's no accident—it's the movie studio's PR team at work to help increase awareness of the new movie.

Feel FREE to Use the Magic Word

In GOB's case, Paul from PR will stage a media event at Bob's House o' GOB to announce the launch of GOB gum and the contest that will bring 50 lucky kids to Orlando to visit the amusement park and get a free vacation. *Free* has been called the magic word in advertising. Everyone sits up and takes notice when you use that word. Don't you? All you have to do is go to GOB's website and try your hand at the online game. See how it all fits together? The promise of a FREE vacation will send parents to the website, and maybe they'll encourage their kids to play the game. Who wouldn't love a FREE family trip to Orlando? And, hopefully, kids will go to the site for the same reason, but also to find out more about the product and about Bob.

This is called "segmentation" in the advertising game. Advertisers want to reach specific segments of the audience, but each audience member is slightly different. Kids are interested in a cool new gum choice, and their parents are interested in a FREE vacation. Getting as many segments of the population as possible to notice GOB increases the chances of a successful product launch.

Much Ado About Everything!

Back at the agency, Penny and Ryan are scrambling to get everything done. Launch day is looming! They need "still" photographs (called stills because they don't move, okay?) of Bob to use in web banners, print advertising, and for "point of purchase" materials. Web banners are those strips you see on the Internet at the top, bottom, and sides of Web pages. Point of purchase materials (POP for short) are signs and

posters placed inside a store near the candy rack or the cash register, the point where you purchase the item.

Think about it the next time you're in a store, and you'll notice them: little "shelf talkers" right there on the shelves, posters hanging overhead, stickers on the floor, signs on the grocery carts. Even billboards along the roads leading to the store. They're everywhere! You're surrounded by advertising. That's why bold images and creative messages are so important: They help attract attention in a world that's cluttered with ads.

Bob Gets Snapped Up

Ryan and Penny select photographer Tina Rogers to shoot the photos of Bob. Harold Hubbard and his parents arrive at Tina's studio, and Harold goes into makeup to become "Bob." The stylists put some "product" in his blond hair to style it, and they put makeup on his face so he'll "pop" in front of the camera. It's the same makeup technique used for actors in television, movies, and plays. It makes a person's face more dramatic, and highlights the eyes and contours of the face so the camera can pick them up better. The stylists put the "Bob" glasses on young Harold Hubbard, and he's magically turned into Bob, standing in front of the camera, surrounded by hot, bright lights. Clouds and blue sky are painted on a backdrop behind him. Tina takes every conceivable angle of Bob: standing, sitting, sideways.

"Up with the arms! Fly, Bob! Fly!" The stylists run in and dab Bob's face with a little powder to keep his forehead from looking too shiny—it's hot under those lights, waving your arms like a bird!

"We need a shot of Bob blowing a bubble," reminds Penny.

"Okay," says Tina. "Bob, act like you're blowing a bubble now!" Bob screws up his face as if he's blowing. "Lift up your arms like you're flying!" Pop, pop, flash, flash.

How Perfection Gets Perfected

But where's the bubble? It's being blown over in the corner by Larry the prop guy. Just like in the TV production, the perfect bubble will be added into the shot later. In print advertising this process is called retouching. Look at the photos in any magazine ad and you'll see that the people look nearly perfect. But you know that people don't really look that way. It's the magic of retouching, where every flaw is smoothed over by a master craftsman, who transfers the shot to a computer and digitally paints out every imperfection. Clients like ACME want the most perfect image possible to represent their product. Retouching is yet another part of the advertising craft. Some people spend every day in front of a computer making other people look fabulous.

This level of perfection also applies to the "product shot." Once Tina has finished shooting Bob, she'll turn her attention to shooting the perfect shot of the GOB gumballs. Using a close-up lens, she'll spend hours shooting the orange and grape gumballs on a white background. That's where Larry the prop man will create his magic. Real GOB gumballs aren't perfectly round, or perfectly smooth. Because they're made on a machine by the millions, each one has a slight imperfection. So Larry creates plastic balls, perfectly round, then paints them to match the exact colors of the real gum. He'll shine them up, and may even coat them with olive oil to make them appear more slick and juicy for the camera. But you wouldn't want to eat one—you'd probably break a tooth!

Olive Oil

Chapter Six

The Launch

Finally the big day has arrived. It's launch day. Packages of new GOB gum are stocked on the shelves of stores from coast to coast. In Los Angeles a poster hangs in a store with a picture of Bob flying and blowing a bubble. In big letters the headline says, "BOB CHEWS GOB! GRAPE! ORANGE! BUBBLES!" Underneath in smaller letters, it reads, "Go to GOB.com and learn to fly! Win a free trip to Bob's House o' GOB in Orlando! Details on pack."

A boy named Alberto stares up at the poster, transfixed by the wacky looking picture of Bob flying along blowing a huge bubble. He eyes the juicy-looking gumballs.

"Come on, Alberto," says his mom, wheeling a cart.

"Wait, Mom," says Alberto. "This gum looks really good!"

Mom turns and looks at the poster. "We need more gum like a hole in the head, Alberto," she says. But by now, Alberto has a pack of GOB in his hand. Mom rolls her eyes...but then looks more closely at the poster. "FREE vacation to Orlando," she reads. "Hmm," she thinks. "Well, maybe we could try just one pack. A FREE vacation for the family would be fun."

Ka-boom! See how it works? Alberto wants the gum. But his mom wants the vacation. This is the clever magic of advertising: two distinct audiences, Alberto and his mom, see something of interest in the message. Slick, huh?

The GOB Effect Unleashed

In Sioux City, Iowa, a 10-year old girl named Shelly is watching her favorite cartoon after school. A commercial pops on, and she sees a funny-looking boy flying along blowing a huge bubble. "I'm Bob, part of the mob that chews GOB!" he shouts. Shelly doesn't think much of it. But then she sees girls her age in a tree. Bob flies over, and the girls say, "Hey Bob, we're part of the mob that chews GOB!" Shelly perks up. "Well, that's sort of cool," she thinks. "This GOB is for girls, too. And look at the size of the bubbles I can blow."

Remember way back when Rona the researcher said girls were more interested in the bubbles? That's why Ryan and Penny and the advertising team made sure to include girls in the commercial and to show them blowing big bubbles. Bingo! Girls like Shelly all over the country notice these scenes and feel included in the GOB message.

The Web Catches Teddy

In Phoenix, Arizona, a 12-year old boy named Teddy is surfing a sports site on the Internet. He sees a web banner with Bob's face on it: "I'm Bob who chews GOB. Grape! Orange! Bubbles!" The banner attracts his attention because Bob looks pretty fun, and because Teddy's favorite gum flavors are grape and orange.

The banner "rolls over," which means it changes to another scene. Now Bob is flying along with hundreds of other kids, all blowing bubbles. "Go to GOB.com and learn to fly. Win a FREE trip to Orlando!"

"Okay," thinks Teddy, "I'll go check it out."

Go to GOB.com and learn to fly.
Win a free trip to Orlando!

He goes to the GOB site and sees that "learning to fly" doesn't really mean he'll find out how to sail through the air by flapping his arms. He knows that's not possible. He sees that it means he can "fly" to Orlando on AIR GOB ONE and meet Bob in person and get a FREE vacation. Cool! Even better, he has to play "Bob's House o' GOB" to win the trip. The game is pretty fun, and so he sends an instant message to his friend, George, across the street.

"Check out GOB.com," the message reads. "There are all these crazy people trying to keep Bob from blowing a bubble. When you get to the roof, watch out for the guy who's hiding behind the chimney with a shovel. I scored 100,000 points. Bet you can't beat that!" Teddy spreads the message to George. This is called "viral messaging." People pass the word along like a cold!

Meanwhile, Back in Orlando...

Ryan and Penny and the agency team fly to Orlando for the "media event" set up by the agency's PR team. Television crews, photographers, and reporters are standing in front of Bob's House o' GOB. Bob throws open the door and greets them. "Welcome to my house! Welcome to Bob's House o' GOB! Come on inside and meet the family!" The house looks exactly like the one in the video game. Bob leads them inside to meet the whole cast of characters from the video game—actors dressed up to play his little sister, his mom and dad, Granny with her knitting, plus the cat and dog. As the cameras roll and flashbulbs pop, the crazy gardener in overalls pops out of the closet with his shovel and growls, "Come on up to the roof, Bob. Let's just see if you can blow one of them GOB bubbles afore I get ye!" It's all pretend, of course, but everyone howls with laughter at the corny cleverness of it all.

"Too cool, dudes," says Ernie the game designer.

GOB Starts Sticking It to Everyone

That night Eddie Lee in Charlotte, North Carolina, surfs the Web and sees a "news" story about Bob's debut for GOB in Orlando. In New York City, Jeanette Villamaria sees a web banner about GOB, clicks on it, and goes to the GOB site. There she sees a link to "Bob's Big Day in Orlando" and clicks on it. She sees Bob, and clicks on the new TV commercial and watches it. In Oklahoma City, Kenny Bowen is watching his favorite TV show about kids in junior high. During a "news break" in the show, there's a video clip of Bob blowing a big GOB bubble while Granny chases him through the house. All over the country, parents tune into a late-night TV talk show. Whoa! There's Bob sitting on the couch, being interviewed. The agency PR team flew him to New York from Orlando on a private jet to get him to the taping that same day! Whenever you see someone on a TV talk show, you can be sure the clever folks doing the advertising arranged the interview.

The next day, newspapers all over the country show photos of Bob in front of his "house" in Orlando. Mr. and Mrs. Nolan, in Milwaukee, Wisconsin, glance over the story at the breakfast table. They're not really interested in gum. That's kids' stuff. But wait just a minute; the headline says, "Old-fashioned bubble gum invites families to Orlando with new-fashioned stunt. FREE vacations!"

"You see this?" Mr. Nolan asks his wife.

"Well, as long as Timmy's chewing gum anyway, maybe he'll win us a FREE trip," she says. Bingo! The advertising has engaged the whole family in the message.

GOB Is Blowing Off the Shelves

The next day kids are lining up to buy GOB. But get this—at a convenience store in Albuquerque, New Mexico, the owner doesn't have any GOB on the shelves. He figured it was just another gum, and

he already has dozens of kinds of gum in stock. "What is this GOB thing?" he says to his candy distributor. "Get me some quick, because kids are lining up to buy it!"

This is called a "pull" strategy in marketing-ese. It means that advertising creates a demand for a product, and that demand compels storeowners to stock the product because so many customers are coming in and asking for it. Advertising creates demand by customers like you. Demand means sales. Sales mean profits for companies. Profits mean jobs for people like your mom and Uncle Max. You really are at the center of advertising. It's made for people like you, and it drives American capitalism. Without demand from customers like you, new ideas and products would never reach the market. It all comes together, over and over, in millions of different ways, for millions of different products, from cell phones to cereal to shampoo to cars.

The Day of Reckoning Is Sweet

The next week Ryan, Penny, Rona, and the account manager have a party at the agency. What a launch it's been! Ernie, the game guru, is there. Pam, the agency producer. Deleon, the TV commercial director. Artie Gomez, who designed the original packaging for GOB. Tina, the photographer. Katie and Monica, the hair and makeup stylists who turned Harold Hubbard into Bob. Paul from the PR department. Larry, the prop guy who made the gumballs look so perfect. Nathan, the retoucher. All the kids from the commercial who hung in their harnesses and "flew."

In walks the client. "On behalf of ACME, I'd like to thank everyone for making the launch of GOB so successful. Remember, six months ago we had nothing but an idea—put grape and orange together so kids could choose which flavor they wanted. We didn't have a name, a package, a commercial…anything. And now we have a huge hit, and we're looking forward to bringing all the video game winners and their families to Orlando."

And They Get Paid to Do This!

Penny and Ryan, the creative team, smile with satisfaction. It's been great fun, teaming up with all their colleagues in the agency. Advertising is a creative business in all sorts of ways, from the people who think up the commercials, to those who buy the media time or space, to those who handle the PR. It takes a team effort—people willing to work together over many long months to turn whispers of ideas into a real advertising campaign that creates products that people enjoy, and profits for businesses that make them. Most people

in the advertising game can't believe they actually get paid to do what they do. It's a wonderful business. But it never stands still.

Advertising lasts only a brief time, and it always needs to be new and fresh and different. When you see advertising on the Internet or on TV, you can be sure that the people behind it are already cooking up the next round, the new campaign, fresh ways to extend the fun for people like you, for whom the advertising is created.

Go Ahead – Take Tonight Off

It's midnight now, and the agency celebration is winding down. The client wraps up his speech: "In conclusion, I'd like to say thanks again for all your hard work and for your brilliant creativity and teamwork. I'm looking forward to...your next set of big ideas."

Ryan and Penny look at each other, smile, and shake their heads. They have been to this movie before.

"See you tomorrow, Penny," says Ryan, giving his creative teammate a big hug.

"It's been really fun," says Penny, hugging Ryan back. She heads home to her apartment and her ever-patient cat, Ed.

"Tomorrow, Ed," she says, scratching his ears, "the fun starts all over again." He curls up on her lap, and they fall asleep on the sofa. Penny dreams of her next big idea. Ed dreams of a world where mice run slowly.

Penny has worked hard to be part of the advertising business. Ed just got lucky. He's not a hard-working cat. He's just a cat.